CAPRICORN H

202

Love, Sex, Career, Wellbeing and Goals

Introduction

Hi Guys,

At last, here is your CAPRICORN HOROSCOPE 2020 with yearly review and monthly forecasts.

2020 is set to be a ground hog year, we have the Saturn Pluto conjunction and three Pluto Jupiter conjunctions all in Capricorn, a solar eclipse at the summer solstice and Jupiter Saturn conjunction at the winter solstice. But what does this all mean for Capricorn?

I aim to do far more astrology on my YouTube channel – Lisa Lazuli Astrology - this year and I want to thank all my subscribers for such excellent support and feedback.

Please join me at my website: lisalazuliastrology.com for podcasts on relationships.
On Facebook: https://www.facebook.com/lisalazuliastrology/
On Instagram: @glisaj
So without any further ago, here it is!

Love from Lisa.

OVERVIEW

"And it all comes down to you"

This can be a lonely year for Capricorn as there are decisions, often quite significant ones, and crossroads that only you can face, and they are significant as the dye will be cast for the next part of your life, not the next phase, no, as the decisions made now will possibly influence the rest of your life.

It's a time where you have to make a break or draw a line, and somethings will get left behind, as they should - just like a snake sheds its skin, or a maybe a better more thrilling example is where superman rips of his suit and reveals his brightly colored superman onesie and shoots off to save the world. Capricorns need to get rid of the shackles that limit your potential and slow you down and in that you can be quite radical, it's time for you to realize your unique destiny.

Now Capricorn is a late bloomer, you take time to understand your talents and realize your worth and potential, however this year, both internal emotional forces as well external economic and social forces, give you opportunities to express yourself and gain power in pursuit of your projects, both new and old.

So, while change is a theme, it's not so much about a personality change, but a shift in attitude where you just see the world differently and make great strides because of that.

This year often includes a sudden disruption or ending to things you previously relied upon, especially external things and you have to learn to look inwards for the answers and strength, as it all comes from within in 2020.

Space X

Capricorns chose some ambitious projects in 2020, and your loved ones may be baffled at some of the choices you make about what you pursue. However, often the project is just the vehicle, it is not so much the outcome you care about, but the focus it gives you and the opportunity to explore aspects of your own personality via this quest. That is why you can pick arduous or even pointless objectives to fixate on.

You want to test yourself, you need to explore your own nature and the boundaries thereof which is why you are a lot more adventurous and eager to explore mentally and psychologically.

The universe expects a lot of Capricorn this year and even if you try to be passive, events will come along to jolt you into action and self-actualization.

It's a very important year in terms of your identity and the way you relate to others, Capricorn can be shy and self-depreciating, but in 2020 you will learn how to 'own it' and to solidify your sense of unique purpose and power.

You have to take your own initiative, no one can hold your hand or explain the route, there is no route yet, that is for you to carve out by yourself. It's a year of very personal achievement - not necessarily success or career advancement, even though these can be helpful perks - not all the changes will even be that obvious to others. Achieving greater self-knowledge and a great deal of satisfaction stems from making personal changes. The growth you undergo will eventually help your relationships run smoother, even if during this phase you are slightly more selfish and self-absorbed.

This year can be a water shed moment in terms of you putting a past relationship and the hurt it represents into an envelope and posting it off to never never land, you have a great capacity to wipe the internal slate clean and start again, and that is very positive if you have been in a relationship or have recently started one, and you feel the shadow of your past lover is ever present. You know when you clean your laptop or smart phone screen and suddenly the text and images are so bright and shiny that it seems like a new experience to use it, life can be like that bright, clean screen for Capricorn if you undergo some internal spring cleaning.

Things you begin this year may blossom in a few years' time or not at all, as not all your new projects are destined for completion, as many are a vehicle for self-unfoldment and are thus stepping stones.

"But its daybreak
If you wanna' to believe
It can be daybreak"

2020 is a year of new opportunities for Capricorn and these will arise in the first few months especially, and yet if these new starts involve new relationships or marriages then all through the year is perfect.

Capricorns have a greater power to create changes in your life this year as your emotional and conscious will are aligned, things just feel right and you can go with your gut as your logical mind is quite happy to agree with the sentiment.

While there is some breakdown and destruction, the renewal happens quite fast. Often in life a door closes and a window opens, but not simultaneously and there can be a rather tense and disheartening period until the new path becomes clear, but this year the new path is often immediately evident, and due to the fall-out from other areas of life, it's quite easy to take the ball and run down that path.

"I get so emotional baby"

Capricorn is a rational character not always in tune with or even respectful of your intuitive feelings as you have an alpha male mentality and can even be quite stiff upper lip. However this year feelings are closer to the surface and they gain strength becoming both a guiding and motivating source. Suddenly your feelings make sense in a contextual sense and you begin to see how logic and intuition is aligning. Your feelings become very useful and will play a far greater role in any new directions you choose. This is not a time when decisions are purely cold hearted and pragmatic, it is rather a time of a wholehearted new embracing of a brand new highway of experiences.

If you have already made a decision which previously made perfect rational sense, the proof will come when you have to live with this decision. It may be that you did not anticipate potential problems as you only made the decision on an intellectual level failing to take account of how you may actually feel. Once you begin to experience the effects on an emotional level, you may feel very differently. This may lead to some U-turns or adjustments to take account of this change of heart. In fact a change of heart is a very good phrase for this year, as often you are swept into a new course of action via a newly discovered strength of feeling. This can leave you quite discombobulated as it can come out of nowhere and you may feel like you are being quite erratic and out of character.

So, you are quite emotional in the way you react and come to conclusions. You may even get a teary eye and be more moved by events or even art, you are more in touch with that impulsive feeling nature rather than having this delayed response where everything is filtered through the head and never even gets to your heart.

It's like your heart is tired of being ignored and is demanding a say, even if you are one of those more emotional Capricorns, and there are some, you will be eager to express and act on those emotions rather than explaining them away.

Often the feelings that surface are important warning signs which can be alerting you to something important. Your gut can be a big ally this year and it will not let you down.

"I found someone to take away the heartache"

This can be a healing year if you have had a great deal of emotional drama or a heart ache, both in terms or relationships or other personal issues. It doesn't really matter if the drama is hot off the press or history, it remains that you can recover psychologically now and draw a line under emotional issues that may have undermined your relationships or burdened you, effectively stunting your emotional growth and stopping you from realizing your full potential in relationships.

You can also break toxic patterns in love. If you are single, you may have compulsively attracted the same personality type, but now you are ready for a brand new brand of relationship, and so if you start dating you may be a little awkward and even tentative, but you can also be like an excited puppy as it is all new to you, you are attracting very different type of woman/man to what you have had before.

Shine on Me

Capricorns are very focused on yourselves and your own needs and you can be moody and distracted in 2020. If you are married or have been in a steady relationship for some time, you may appear less of the reliable, stalwart companion you usually are. You can be more whimsical, you may be more sullen or withdrawn and you could demand more freedom. You may have a classic case of midlife crisis, probably because you tend to question more and you feel restless and less satisfied with routines.

Here is the crux, Capricorns mature later than others emotionally, they tend to be brought up to be restrained, strong and reliable and to suppress their more expansive or subjective instincts, however in 2020 you begin to discover and explore your feeling nature and this changes many of your responses. Sometimes you lack emotional maturity and are selfish in seeking to meet your newly discovered needs, but you find it hard to exercise the restraint which you have in the past, and you can feel quite liberated. While you may test your partner's patience, you will emerge a more rounded person, possible more sympathetic as well.

Breakthtu or Break Free?

Uranus brings a great deal of creativity, spontaneous energy and rebelliousness to Capricorn. You feel the need to be a little wild and express yourself free from the disapproving eyes of peers or of your partner. You begin to think the usual boundaries of your life are no longer a good fit for you, they need to change and others need to accommodate your newfound outlooks.

You are consumed with discovering your own identity and chipping away all the parts of yourself you feel were only added to conform, or even get ahead. Typical of this period, can be the example of a Capricorn who had worked hard and kept your head down and suddenly, you are in the position where you no longer has to cow tie to others, you can set the agenda and express your ideas or philosophy with authority. When you get just a little freedom either in terms of management, creativity or romantically (where you are newly single) you can go a little crazy for a time as you are not very discriminating and just want to grab at everything or anything.

Of course not everyone is going to get on board your free spirited Capricorn Express, it's very much about you isn't it? What is in it for others, they may feel like they are left holding the baby quite literally or shouldering the responsibility? However, this is an exciting time for you and yet it is not free of inner turmoil either as your old defense mechanisms and internal voices are going to be grumbling away, telling you to calm down.

I guess we all have a rebellious phase, where we just want to throw away the rules and find out how it feels. That is where Capricorn is at, but you will soon return to many of your old ways and rules if you find they are valid, but some will be gone for good. Your rebelliousness is not about being bad, it's about being more creative and inspired and having a life philosophy that says 'you can' rather than ' you can't'. As a Capricorn, you have always battled fear, but now you are more positive, despite any of the major changes that may go on in your life, and opportunities abound.

In relationships, you are looking for fun and you enjoy surprises, you may be ready for different styles of foreplay or new ways to get into the mood. You are more open minded and your sexual interest is quickly aroused, so if life in the bedroom had become dull and you and your partner had stopped seeing each other as sexual beings, that could be about to change.

You will be quite surprised by the sort of women/men you attract this year as your need for free spirited, even eccentric types, reflects an inner need you have to break some new ground and be free. Relationships have an unpredictable quality and it's not clear whether what begins this year has the legs to last or is part of a development phase you are going through. However, there is a powerful mental rapport and an intriguing mental relationship that develops with your girl/boyfriends this year and that has every chance of lasting and providing a lifetime of friendship.

Moonraker

Capricorns are in an innovative frame of mind and this year is excellent for invention and also technological pursuits. You may receive a grant to do research or funding for social projects which are futuristic. Your work is far more likely to be linked to emerging technology like 5g, driverless cars, smart cities or new laws connected to media.

You will most likely have brand new opportunities at work which will bring you into contact with different people, who may well inspire a whole new outlook in you. Your whole focus in terms of career direction will change, you may well move to work in a different industry or perhaps changes in the wider economy mean your current job will never be the same. The world is changing fast and Capricorn seem to be at the cutting edge, and this is where money can be made.

Your life is far more dynamic and changes that happen are liberating for you, but they happen fast and often there is almost too much choice and so mistakes can be made, yet you learn fast.

Again, you often find yourself in unchartered territory where there are no rules yet, perhaps few facts, and where you have little experience, which is why you will learn to use your intuitive perceptions and rely on your gut.

You may get a new boss who totally shakes things up and encourages you to make bold decisions, often lurking somewhere this year is a trailblazing mentor who inspires you to cut loose.

You may achieve sudden fame or acclaim for your ideas, or even your crisis management as you can be a key player when the chips are down.

If you are in the creative industry, this can be year you get your break. Opportunities come fast and slip through your grasp just as fast, but like buses they keep coming along this year.

"Wired close to you"

If you have been in a relationship for a short time, this year may see a few breaks in the relationship. You may spend time apart due to work, but often you both decide you need space or a cooling off period and it can work very well if you both need to straighten out priorities and get some relationship mojo back.

If single, you can have on-again and off-again love relationships, partly because you fall in love fast, get quite excited, but then get the feeling that things are moving too fast and you back off, not because you no longer fancies the person, but because it's all a bit of a blur and you are feeling confused. Now usually when someone claims they are confused, it's just a massive rouge and a wimpy way out, but Capricorn is actually genuinely confused by your relationships and emotions this year and so you can be taken you at your word.

Now Capricorn have a freedom closeness dilemma this year. You crave warmth and quality companionship, but you balk at the idea of restriction and let's be honest if you want a kind, committed companion, they will generally want some form of commitment or regularity to the relationship, but you are not in the mood for commitment. You may complain that you just cannot meet the right kinda girl/guy, truth is, the girls/guys are out there but you are just not settling for one, as deep down you are enjoying your freedom, even though it can be a little lonely.

So on-again off-again love works for you as you get a taste of both. The worst problem is that you may be convinced you can have it all, you may assume that you can be a best buddy, an occasional lover and a delightful date all at the same time, when we know it never works like that. Love is a little like cocaine, you can't just take it or leave it, once you get into it and you're hooked, it's painful to walk away. So how does this all breakdown, you may be super keen to get into a relationship and may fall in love fast, but once the initial whirl wind settles, you may become moody and disruptive and look to have more time alone, while keeping your partner on a string. Or, you flirt and keep potential partners at arm's length while you play the field. You can be quite an exciting prospect if your partner too is restless romantically and looking for a relationship that offers stimulating conversation, a vibrant rush of emotion and tenderness, without a feeling of need or control on either side.

Prosperity

Venus brings prosperity this year. There are sudden chances to earn money and often sums of money come to you unexpectedly. You may make a few unusual purchases this year, you could suddenly decide to invest in art or bitcoin, or maybe you will do something financially for the very first time.

This should be a time of more comfort in terms of money due to increased opportunity, however you should take nothing for granted as by the nature of work this year, there may be more risk involved.

Extra money this year often does not involve more hours, it can be the result of better use of your skills or your ability to be more daring and go beyond your usual limits. As stated before, greater earning potential can be linked to switching to an emerging industry ripe for profit.

Profit often comes by not playing it safe, that does not mean you take risks, but rather that some bridges may have to be burned and some old contacts in your network may not be that happy. Often financial opportunities and the success they bring costs you friends or alienates some of the people you used to work with, but c'est la vie.

The powerful advantage in this year, is in your ability to make your own dreams come true and not to have to work with others or help others fulfil themselves. You have enormous potential for your own identity defining moments that come by achieving success in your own right.

Dreams and destiny seem just that little bit more real and reachable this year and you have a mindset that is one big green light and no one is going to rain on this parade.

Children

Children living at home could be experiencing monumental changes in their lives which make them more unpredictable, and which requires great tolerance and an open mind from you. Kids tend to surprise or even shock you in 2020 and often you just have to go with the flow and embrace what they are doing, or support them. In the longer term, you may be able to have some influence over their state of mind, but this year things may be out of your control and you just have to stay abreast of things, keep communication open, and hang in there until the dust settles and all can be straightened out.

Children can be more disruptive and events around them can be unsettling. However, it works both ways as it may be that some of the decisions about work and relationships that you makes have a knock on effect on their lives which they are not happy about and they rebel.

In general, you have to treat your kids, or your step kids, like adults (as long as they are not too young obviously) and respect their views and give the more credit for understanding what is going on. The worst thing you can do is underestimate them, they understand more than you know and they deserve to have explanations and to be consulted on big decisions. Don't disregard their intellectual input, but that doesn't mean they should rule the roost either. Kids this year respond better to reason than to exclusion.

If your children have been subjected to upheaval or school changes recently, stay in close communication with them, they may need more support than you know. While kids do need extra freedom this year, sometimes excessive rebelliousness and contrariness are a call for help and understanding.

Matters of the Mind

Capricorn can be quite private and distracted in 2020. You are spending a great deal of time processing information and this can pertain to your inner conflicts or research connected to new lines of work.

Often you seek extra work or throw yourself into some mentally challenging or absorbing activity to avoid dealing with your feelings, which as you know can bubble up and overpower you this year. However, at other times you crave deeper understanding and may seek psychological guidance. You are bound to do this secretly, via books etc, rather than by visiting a shrink or going to a group as that is way too embarrassing, but nonetheless you are more eager to explore esoteric issues and edgy concepts that will aid your understanding. In some cases you may visit a psychic or mystic.

Jupiter brings with it a philosophical urge and this year Mercury is in a rather mystical position for Capricorn which encourages deeper contemplation of meanings, dreams and symbols, you are more concerned about your place in the grand scheme of things and the meaning of your life. This does contribute to this restless dissatisfaction you have and it also makes you quickly bored. Capricorn is much more interested in the bigger picture and the longer term perspective this year and you can be a little careless with details as they don't interest you.

You are rather scatty in the first part of the year and will miss important dates, so you may need Alexa to be your talking diary as you are far more random.

Now while in the first part of the year you are more introspective and perhaps not that eager to chat about feelings, in the second part of the year, you open up especially in marriage and long term relationships and are very willing to express yourself and get feedback from others.

This can be a very good year for you to have psychoanalysis or therapy as your feelings are close to the surface and you have a genuine intellectual desire to delve deep and understand yourself and your relationship dynamics.

"And I wonder why we hold on with tears in our eyes"

This is a powerful and poignant year in marriage as Capricorn is going through several transitions both at work and personally, and this will test relationships especially if you are with cardinal sign too.

You certainly have a taste for self-expression and this becomes an obsession which could easily, as I have said, be compared to a midlife crisis, as you are experimental and hungry for thrills, however it's deeper than a crisis, it is a necessary part of your life story which really does need editing and reworking. This is an ideal opportunity for you to shake off limiting beliefs, grievances or negative internal voices so that you can live a more authentic life.

Relationships can get very much stronger by virtue of your ability to accept things about yourself less judgmentally and access a broader range of emotions. There is the chance that you guys may talk about things you never have before as you open up and new understanding can be reached accompanied via far more tenderness and a deeper connection. You could say 'what doesn't kill the relationship makes it stronger' this year, but that sounds quite alarming as it doesn't not have to be that bad, indeed there are loads of positives.

Priorities often change in love, what used to important can now be usurped by new prerogatives. What was taken for granted is now cherished, there can be a rediscovery in love of what really counts, and with that, a sense of the uniqueness of your journey together and the bond that has developed after all that you have been through. Capricorn can become obsessed with appearances and keeping up with the Jones', however this year you are grateful and joyful of the quirky and atypical things which make your relationship great, convention goes out the window and you see the innate beauty in what is imperfect yet intrinsic to your love.

Sex

This is a year when you want your sex life to get outside the box, you are frustrated by what is conventional or repetitive and your whole value system around sex may be about to change as you are eager for some new sexual experiences and you have quite an appetite too.

If you have any proclivities or fantasies, this is the year you may seek to test or live these out. You are less moralistic, and so options tend to expand.

In sex, you desire more excitement, and so whatever increases adrenalin makes for good love making. You are not very visual in love, it's not about looks or ambiance, it's more about challenge. To turn you on, your partner needs to stimulate your competitive nature, stoke your ego, challenge you in some way via a sexual games or totally surprise you. Sex in brand new places and forbidden places works, (don't break any laws guys lol, I don't want to read about you on the news), spontaneous unplanned sex in new surroundings also works well. Make your partner look for you, make him/her undress you blindfolded or just with their teeth, make foreplay part of the game or challenge and definitely make time for love.

Spread your Wings

This year is marked by increased self-awareness on an emotional and spiritual level and a desire for self-expression and self-actualization. You are more aware of what you have to offer on a personal and professional level and so you are harder to push around and more demanding in wanting your fair dues back. You value yourself more and thus you change your approach to love.

Conclusion

You have more belief in yourself and although there is crisis, you are quick to see the positive therin and to spot escape route from damaging long term situations and so this is an 'every cloud has a silver lining' sort of year. At work you will have more scope to express your ideas and go into exciting new fields where there is far more potential long term.

This year is one of emerging; let me be honest the past few years have probably been tough for Capricorn with a great deal of soul searching, disappointment and even unhappiness and yet the sun is about to come out. Part of the year is dealing honestly with emotions that suddenly come to the surface. It is almost as if you feel instinctively that you are reaching the end of an important and yet crises ridden phase of your life, and you need to release all those emotions that were on hold while you were patiently and determinedly dealing with what was important. You can be tearful and reflective, in some cases you are moody as you are emotionally exhausted, but this is a processing year (especially the first half) after which you are ready to talk and relate more openly than ever before in love and with a greater understanding of yourself which can only help relating in love.

So get ready for brand new directions and a boost to your worldly ambitions and be ready for a more honest and open hearted relationship that is more reflective of your needs and a lot closer. This year demands an open mind and I think you more than ready for that; it is a year of brand new chapters, new possibilities and putting the past firmly where it belongs, as part of a closed chapter.

New relationships should be enjoyed and lived in the moment; this is not a year for relationship planning as nothing can be set in stone, the energy says, 'listen to your heart, live in the moment, forget convention ,dam what anyone says', so love and live authentically.

Spiritually this is also a key year for Capricorn, not only do you begin to learn to listen to your heart and your intuition, you are more aware of a grand plan and you have a renewed faith and a sense of destiny. You can begin to take quite an interest in spiritual, religious or esoteric concepts, as suddenly your dreams are vivid and coincidences keep telling you that there is something going on, beyond logic and reason, and you had better pay attention. It can be quite a lucky year, but is it really luck or are things just beginning to click as your awareness expands, and you are more open to inspiration and the calling of the universe.

JANUARY 2020

Life

There is a great big conjunction between the Sun, Mercury, Saturn and Pluto this January making it a highly significant month for all star signs, what can Capricorn expect?

The force is with you and you have the power to make brave and bold decisions that will have a great deal of influence on the rest of your life. At the root of changes you make now is the pressing need to have more control over your life and to purge yourself of what has become useless and outdated. Capricorn are embracing both the possible and impossible in a wide spectrum of choices, and some of what you do is an uncharacteristic leap in the dark and yet you feel that you have to take some risks in order to test yourself.

Your personality is more powerful and magnetic and you will attract strong and influential people as friends and also as enemies as you are upping your game, and there is more at stake in your life and which makes some issues more contentious.

Money

Right now you may have to get by with less; it could be helpful to redeploy your money to the places where it garners the biggest return as you will not be able to cover all bases. You may have to make some cutbacks and you could get close to credit limits, reducing your flexibility in the short run, however you are encouraged to eliminate all unnecessary expenses or activities to bring about a stronger long term position.

This is time were you have to be ruthless and so know what needs to go and get rid of it and don't look back. There is no time to be idealistic and sentimental, you gain by taking the tough decisions and building, in some cases, from the bottom up.

Health

Emotional fluctuations are the biggest health issue as your energy goes faster when you get angry or upset and emotional situations take it out of you.

This month is one of creative change where you will have the inner resolve and also the tenacity to reform circumstances in your daily life that have become troublesome, time wasting, or intolerable. Often, you have had to put up with something for some time, and now it's the month when you will put your foot down and say, "No more!"

Romance

While existing relationship status quos are challenged, new love can blossom in unexpected places and often via strange coincidences. Love right now feels meant to me and for that reason it moves quickly, Capricorn are attracted to Scorpio, Pisces, Leo and Cancer this month.

Hidden ego tensions will come to the fore in newly formed relationships and if jealousy is a problem it will surface now. Arguments can stem from unexpressed sexuality or a feeling that you are not being put first. Capricorns need to ensure that their love partner feels important, feels listened to or understood; you cannot up the ante sexually if you are neglecting other parts of the relationship.

Love and Marriage

Relationships can be quite fraught as the energies within you are powerful but not always streamlined and so you can be irritable and uneasy. You have to watch out for being passive aggressive as you are ostensibly non-confrontational, and yet you may invoke, subconsciously, conflict with your partner. However, conflict no matter how it comes about can be creative and helpful as you and your partner break new ground. Relationships new and old need strong and tangible signs of commitment and loyalty and so relationships which involve a partner who is distant or who desires freedom will have the highest levels of angst.

Sex

What is needed in relationships are deep and meaningful conversations and sharing of fears and issues close to your heart – this can reinforce intimacy and closeness and can allay fears which lead to insecurity and the need to control and perceive a need for jealousy.

Career

You may have some doubts about your abilities; you should not underestimate your skills or experience or put yourself down. The self-doubt (either you are feeling you lack experience or perhaps are not as qualified) you are experiencing can actually spur you on to be more determined or hard working to prove yourself, and so the doubt drives you on in a positive way.

Although your desire nature is strong right now and you have an immense amount of emotional energy, you are up against universal forces, evolutionary trends and often a tide of social change – that is why you can get further if you go with the flow; fighting against it is impossible.

You have a great deal of persistence and deep reserves of emotional energy, and this can help you endure storms and keep you focused. You are very single-minded and not in the mood to let things get on top of you, which means that no matter what, you will achieve this month, even though it will not come easily.

Key Dates

The moon wanes between the 10th and 24th making this your consolidation and building phase, make sure you complete projects and attend to details systematically. Prior to the 10th and after the 24th are better for implementing brand new plans and launching projects. After the 24th is favorable for property and home improvements as well as large family events. Short trips away for both relaxation and culture are also a great idea. After the 24th is an appropriate time to deal with those in authority or with government; you can have success when taking on the big guys and you may also gain recognition. Starting a brand new career is favored; you may be headhunted or selected via an arduous and long process.

FEBRUARY 2020

Life

Mercury goes retrograde on the 16th or February, meaning some frustration and delays as well as misconceptions in love. Avoid making promises as you are not actually that sure about what you feel about emotional matters right now. Your needs are changing, and you don't want to be backed into a corner. Capricorn are known for being reliable, but that often creates a great deal of pressure for you as you hate to let people down. So this month do not be afraid to say, "I don't know" or "I'll get back to you'," stop feeling the compulsion to be decisive and precise, let others wait and be patient for a change, and reserve the right to change your mind.

Money

Mercury retrograde period causes delays in negotiations over contracts, bank transfers, cheques clearing and payments. Debtors may be slower to pay up. Be cautious about who you extend credit to. Make sure you monitor cash flow carefully and allow for unexpected expenses.

Send any payments registered mail and make sure you get people to sign for any valuable item you deliver. Be very clear on terms and conditions when you purchase new services, check carefully how much time you have to cancel and apply for a full refund if the service is unsuitable. Look out for guarantee and warrantee expiry dates.

Streamline, cut waste and cancel services or product lines which cost more in time or inputs than they contribute to margin.

This is a lucky money month and there may be good news in terms of new orders, new clients or money making opportunities in the pipeline.

Health

This month is one of health related research and it may not even be your own health, it may be your partner's, or even your pet's health which you need to know more about in order to be of help.

Knowing more about a health issue is initially confusing, but you should persist as it will all make sense eventually and the knowledge gained can be quite empowering.

Romance

Capricorn are in a very idealistic frame of mind which can make you more open, more romantic and that can help love to develop quickly as your guard is down. However, you are not that pragmatic in love, and while in theory love conquers all, in practice the material things do create hurdles and love is not an uninterrupted spiritual experience. So, what I am saying, is that you can become infatuated and you may begin a relationship that has enormous emotional benefit, but which cannot be actively pursued in the short term. For example, you may begin a friendship online with a person who has no financial means to travel to see you in the short term and you may fall deeply in love with this person, which can present frustration. You may fall for someone who is married or attached and who cannot leave her/ his current partner yet. So there is love, potentially great love, but frustration and delay.

Love and Marriage

Capricorn have a desire to be the center stage right now and you can become frustrated when your partner does not give you his full attention or admiration; this is why you can become annoyed at any hint of him/her being 'too' friendly with another. It would be healthy for you to cast your net wider; your desire for attention may be too intense for one person to fulfil.

You may argue about matters to do with the home and family and often things are highly charged and not very productive and so best to avoid debate and find practical and constructive things to do together.

If debate and healthy discussion are alive and well in your relationship, this can be a stimulating time, but perhaps a trying own if you partner is very sensitive and not up for some frank conversation.

Sex

Sexually you are a bit of an animal right now as you may need more physical affection, sex and also mental stimulation than usual – yes

Capricorn are quite a handful and you enjoy partners who challenge you and push your buttons, you are tuned on by sexually and intellectually provocative partners.

Career

Mercury goes retrograde on the 16th or February after which you may find any long haul travel, legal matters and business conducted with people or companies in other countries problematic.

Knowing relevant law is essential and you may have to investigate more deeply and get expert advice, as the details matter and you cannot afford to be unclear or even unconcerned about these legal technicalities especially where they relate to international law, copy write, data protection and internet regulation.

Intensive training may be needed for a new job you have begun and you are faced with some criticism at the start, but don't be demoralized as you are doing better than you think and some mistakes are part of the process.

Key Dates

The Mercury retrograde period is also a time for added planning and caution in relation to long distance travel and import, export agreements. It's not a good time to outsource and you need to supervise staff carefully. Read contracts very carefully and delay large purchases if possible as you may well get a better deal next month. Negotiations may stall and there are often delays or mistakes in terms of paperwork, transactions and business information systems. The moon wanes from the 9th to the 23rd marking a time for completion and implementation, after the 23rd is best for brand new projects especially in relation to property and self-employment. After the 23rd is also great for restaurant launches and businesses related to green energy. Post the 23rd is not good for marriage or getting engaged.

MARCH 2020

Life

Mercury goes direct from the 9th of March, meaning that the problems of Mercury retrograde last month begin to improve quite quickly. This month, after the 9th, is excellent for new business, business travel, management initiatives and pursuing new ideas. This month is ideal for both investigation and brainstorming, and it pays to explore new ideas with colleagues and advisors, be more daring and expansive and start to contemplate what is possible and then research it. This is a month of seeding opportunity, as often what seems daunting or even impossible is actually just a long series of steps and each individual step is totally possible.

This is an excellent time for a spring clean, you benefit psychologically by decluttering and beautifying your home and you may feel the need for new curtains, paintings, furniture etc. to create a fresh feeling ahead of the new season. You can kick start emotional renewal by changing your surroundings: psychological change does not always have to begin on the inside, it can begin on the outside by being proactive about your lifestyle and actively making choices which improve life in practical ways.

Money

Delays and problems with financial matters will be resolved after the 9th when Mercury is direct, contracts can be finalized and discussions about money proceed smoothly.

An excellent month for budgeting, doing financial forecasting and analysis. You have a better grasp of what is possible and what you will need for any major project, making this an excellent time to put together the pieces of a new venture and start the ball rolling.

Look at new money making ideas, even if you are employed, there are additional money making streams which you can find now.
A good time to invest in art or fine jewelry.

Health

This is the best time of year for Capricorn to make new health resolutions.

Initiate new fitness regimes, start a new diet, or begin to learn a new sport. It helps to have targets, and you enjoy competitive activities and so make sure you go for fitness or sports that bring out that competitive spirit and get your adrenalin going.

You are quickly bored and so you need challenge and variety, so do not invest in expensive gym equipment or a membership package if you are likely to get bored with it quickly.

Add garlic, onions, leeks and chili peppers to your food as they are good for you right now. Curries and other spicy food can be invigorating.

Romance

This is a rather sensible, pragmatic time for you and you may now have a new take on romances which are rather tricky or complicated. However, you don't want to ditch these romances, you would rather figure out how to make then work and you can spend a great deal of time unraveling relationship issues, working on solutions to the practical issues that face you, and being really rational in order to balance some of the emotional turmoil which inevitably comes with new relationships now.

A greater desire to communicate means that relationships started online, or which have a great deal of written communication continue to progress, and are very rewarding.

Humor is very important in new relationship as they can get too sentimental and a little heavy at times, and you need to highlight the funny side of your dilemmas.

Love and Marriage

You are very self-directed and often preoccupied this month. This is not necessarily a tender or loving month, it's more about getting stuff done. You are highly motivated and even a little bossy and can become frustrated by a lackluster or passive partner.

You may be too busy at work or with your business to give your partner or love life full attention, or you may be very engaged in home life, but not in terms of being affectionate i.e. you may be doing DIY or attending to family members or even arranging family events.

This is a busy time within the family and home, and you are at the forefront, however although you are enthusiastic, in your zeal to get things done, you can be impatient and brusque with your partner.

Sex

You have high desire but little patience, you enjoy fast spontaneous sex and too much emotion can turn you off. You rather enjoy masturbation as often you can satisfy yourself more effectively.

Career

This is an excellent month for leadership, so be bold, be daring and set new targets and goals to aim for. A great time to apply for a new job with greater responsibility and more freedom to manage projects. An excellent month to become self-employed or start a new business from scratch.

Prior to the 9th, tie up loose ends, complete anything pending, and settle debts, then clear the deck to make way for new projects. The period after the 9th is the time to be flexible and innovative, new opportunities come when you follow leads and react fast to new information which comes your way. Don't sit still and plod away, there are better more productive avenues for your time.

This is a good period to find new suppliers and invest in equipment which can improve efficiency.

If you are in catering, hospitality or tourism this is an excellent month to run promotions and reach out to your regular customers with discount opportunities and rewards.

Self-employment is more rewarding this month and you may feel less pressure and more of a sense of fulfillment.

Key Dates

Mercury goes direct on the 9th indicating that communication, short distance travel, sales contracts and transactions begin to flow again with fewer hiccups. The moon wanes from 9th until the 24th making this a time of diligence and application, after the 24th is best for career moves, job applications and interviews. This post 24th period is also great for PR and public speaking engagements. New management directions are favored. This is not the best time for major changes to your body i.e. cosmetic surgery, dental implants or getting tattoos.

APRIL 2020

Life

The key word this month is courage: the measure of success, achievement, excitement and fulfilment in our lives is more proportional to courage than anything else, and so take the plunge, listen to your heart and do not let anything hold you back. Most of us know what it is we need to be happier or more successful, however we make excuses and find negatives to deter us. This is the time to be brave, ignore the negative voices both inside yourself and outside, and act on your instincts, take control of your destiny and feel the flame inside you burn brighter.

Often life's struggles diminish our inner fire, our spirit, but it's never destroyed, it's there just waiting for the oxygen of change and fresh ideas to come, and then it roars again and you are alive - that can happen now. Help your flame reignite by saying no to restrictive practices and excessive obligation.

Money

An excellent month for money making through your own initiatives. This is a busy and highly productive time for fledgling businesses, new ventures and new business lines.

Ventures which start now take off fast and activity is hectic and unpredictable. Investment in high teq industries is also favored.

Sportsman can be very successful financially and any business connected to sports equipment, training, clothing, or a sporting venue can be very profitable.

Opportunities come quickly and demand decisiveness and some guts, it's a very demanding time and your management skills are stretched.

Health

It's easier to achieve your health goals this month as you are more motivated and you will get ample encouragement. This is a perfect month to join support groups or attend meetings to help with your weight loss, addictions or fitness, as you tend to achieve more with group support or within a team.

This is a perfect time to tackle negative conditioning or trauma bonding, you need to understand your compulsion to act in a self-destructive way when faced with certain situations and your tendency to self-sabotage. This is a good time to recognize these patterns and work to uncover their source, which may be in a childhood experience or previous relationship.

Romance

An excellent month socially, and you are able to add many new friends to your circles. In terms of work and your non work activities, there are more events to attend and life has greater variety bringing new romantic opportunities.

Relationships should be light and carefree this month, keep your options open and do not get too heavily involved. Take a 'wait and see attitude', enjoy dating or just going out in groups and chatting to potential partners. There may well be more than one person who catches your eye so don't grab the first to come along. A time to be a social butterfly, even though I know it's not necessarily Capricorns style, however you can benefit from being open but non-committal. Communication is key to any relationship which begins now, and so if you click mentally, that is an excellent clue of compatibility, more so than sexual attraction.

Love and Marriage

Capricorn need more space in relationships right now than you realize. Things could be becoming intense and lacking in perspective and you may need a short break mid-month, or later in the month to clear your head.

There can be disruptions which disrupt the usual flow of events or the routine in your relationship, but this can present an ideal opportunity for a rethink. You guys may be on a course that, if honest, neither of you believe in, and now is the time to take advantage of any sudden happenings or even arguments, to voice concerns or broach tricky subjects that don't often come up.

The universe may throw a spanner in the works and the best laid plans may come to nothing, however this is often lucky in the long run and may set you both on a better course ultimately.

Sex

Sexlife is complicated and there are some deep and possibly troubling issues to confront. You may encounter themes of control and you may feel that you are being emotionally manipulated. You have to be alert in intimate situations and should keep your boundaries up, don't be an open book, keep something in reserve. This is not a good time to be totally open with a new partner or with your spouse, secrets are often self-protection, don't feel bad for having them.

Career

This month is ripe for networking opportunities and you should take advantage of any professional conferences or get-togethers. A good time to attend trade fairs, exhibitions and seminars where you can touch base with those in your industry and hear the latest developments.

Friends are more supportive of your aims and it's a good time to be vocal about your ambitions or goals as you never know who has the key to your success, perhaps a friend has a piece of information or a contact which can be invaluable to you.

This month is ideal for longer term planning and brainstorming of new ideas for your business or for your career, you are restless and ready for a new challenge. Think ahead of the curve and be open-minded as the best opportunities right now are the more radical or controversial ones.

Key Dates

The moon wanes from 7th until the 22nd making this a time of diligence and application, after the 22nd is best for your new projects and for creative ventures and launches. After the 22nd is excellent for creative writing, short distance travel by sea, water sports and PR. Fields like graphic design, the visual arts and work which requite solitude are favored. An excellent time for work which needs inspiration. Work in the pharmaceutical and alterative medicine field is profitable.

MAY 2020

Life

An excellent month to set the record straight and you gain by being direct with others. Honesty is the best policy. Life is hectic but dynamic and this is a great time to initiate and step on the gas.

Jupiter turning retrograde in your first house brings some unusual perspectives and often a slightly different slant on morality, this month you can be quite controversial or perhaps a better way to put it is, bluntly honest in your perspectives, you cut through what is fake and go to what really counts in the debate often making others uncomfortable with the clarity you bring.
You have quite crucial insights into events and you have vision and yet your own vision can be at odds with what everyone else is going along with – you could be the party pooper who says, "Hey, we all need to sober up and get a grip here!" While you are right on many issues, it could be a while until others come round to you way of thinking, which could be somewhat of an 'inconvenient truth'.
Your own experience is your best guide right now; so no matter what others are saying about XYZ, if XYZ never worked before for you, it won't now and so use the past as your best guide to the future.
Even when things are going well, you will not be complacent – you plan meticulously and keep a beady eye on proceedings taking nothing for granted. You take great care to think about the domino effect of your actions and you are mindful of long term repercussions.

Money

Major financial transactions or the taking out of loans should be avoided.

There is a lack of clarity financially and you should take a back seat and observe both the markets and your own cash flow, as it may fluctuate this month unexpectedly. You are not quite certain of anything right now, you have a vague feeling that something significant is going to develop, but it's too soon to say what yet.

You are inclined to be hasty and to act on instinct this month however, your impatience may mean you act on instincts without understanding what they are actually telling you, which is why you need to sit tight until you are clear what your gut is actually conveying to you.

Health

This month is excellent for establishing some positive new habits, however you need to ease yourself in and you should not go cold turkey, or try anything too extreme. If you currently eat meat every day, don't go straight to being vegan, rather reduce red meat as a first incremental step as May is not geared for a massive dietary change or indeed a sudden uptake of strenuous exercise.

It's an excellent month to get a new pet, as animals can be good therapy.

Joining a fitness group is a good move as social exercise is likely to appeal to you more and you will have an added incentive to keep at it.

Drink more water, especially when you wake up first thing and last thing before bed.

Romance

This is not the best month for brand new relationships to begin, but you should be especially cautious in starting romance or even flirting with employees. In any relationship where there is a duty of care, be very wary of any feelings which are developing. It is likely that someone who you act in a professional capacity for i.e. a patient, or client, or a person you give care to, can develop feelings for you which can make your professional relationship complicated.

Love is often unrequited this month, and it's probably you who are the subject of unwanted attention from a person who you either do not fancy at all, or who you may have initially liked, but quickly went off.

In new relationships started this year, your patience and depth of feeling is tested as you begin to adjust to each other and some flexibility and sacrifice is needed.

Love and Marriage

This can be a month or bickering and arguing over trivial matters, however, these are just signs that communication has become unfit for purpose and that it's an aspect of your relationship that requires renewal. Stop dropping hints, making snide remarks or being vague, say what needs to be said and ask for what you feel is due to you. This is a good month to get the balance of give and take back into the relationship and sometimes just letting your partner know about the daily chores he/she is neglecting, or the habits that have become annoying, can go a long way to remedying the situation. It's about creating awareness of where respect is missing, or has been lost and addressing that.

A very good month to start a new diet or fitness regime with your partner. Going vegetarian or starting training together can be a bonding experience which helps open a new chapter for you both.

Sex

Unfulfilled sexual or romantic passions can be channeled into superb artistic work or poetry and music. You are wildly creative and I mean wildly as you are ready to throw convention (or even a television) out of the window and shout "rock 'n roll" as you embrace the creative process with gusto.

Career

This month it's a scatter attack approach where even with the best will you cannot focus on one thing, but you rather have to race from thing to thing either solving problems or taking advantage of opportunities. It's a fast paced month and it can be productive, however it's more about many small steps adding up to something significant, rather than one great leap.

You are impatient and have to watch out for being a little abrupt, remember to appreciate others and give a few words of encouragement here and there as you are not at your most diplomatic.

It's a very good month for fast learning either of facts or skills as you are very alert and receptive to new information. You can also debate with greater power as you have an intellectually forceful manner, although you have to try and be constructive not just argumentative.

Try and reduce commuting and make better use of video calls and hangouts, as traveling short distance is a massive time sink, and the frustration can be often avoided.

Key Dates

Venus retrograde from the 13th of May to the 25th of June is not an opportune time for marriage or starting a new relationship. The moon wanes from 7th the until the 22nd making this a time of patience and planning, after the 22nd is best for your new projects and for important business dates and launches. After the 22nd is perfect for creative projects, medical training and careers like dance. Visualization and the honing of psychic powers is also favored. New businesses related to mind, body spirit do well.

JUNE 2020

Life

Mercury goes retrograde from the 18th of June in Cancer, and this can complicate negotiations, mediation and legal matters. This retrograde period also causes more misunderstandings in your interpersonal relationships and so you have to make a bigger effect to be clear and concise.

This is not an ideal month for long haul travel, which can end up being more exorbitant than you anticipated. Travel does not always bring the rewards it promised in terms of business opportunities or pleasure.

You may be very involved in your children's education and their exams or schedule can cause you greater stress. There is a lot to pack in this month and being organized and keeping promises is vital. It's not necessarily easy to keep your word as you are pulled in many different directions and have conflicting priorities, however you can only do what you can do, and so cut yourself some slack.

Money

A good month for property negotiations and also for investing in property; but you need to know what you want and to have check lists that are detailed and which you use to help you negotiate. While Capricorn are ready to make deals, you need to be more certain of what you want to achieve and what you need from these deals.

Capricorn have important hunches and perceptions that go beyond logic and they can help you to make timely and important decisions. Often great ideas or eve warnings come to you in dreams.

Health

This is a good month to deepen your understanding of the psychological issues which impact health. Loneliness is a key issue for Capricorn who often feel lonely even in relationships or in a family, which is why last month and this, getting a pet or even interacting with animals can be therapeutic.

Capricorn benefit from social and community activities which give you a sense of purpose and which can also accelerate psychological healing. Often helping others, empowers us in our own life and gives us strength, and Capricorn should reach out this month to experience this.

New diets continue to progress, but health matters should not be rushed, keep a steady pace and remember to taper rather than cutting anything out all in one go. A small amount of caffeine and sugar is beneficial even if you are dieting or detoxing.

Romance

Online and internet romance can become quite a distraction and Capricorn may spend far more time chatting to potential partners late at night, at work and while traveling, on social media. These secret relationships which develop in the cyber world have an odd fascination for you and can be quite addictive. You should however be careful about what you believe or reveal, as your guard comes down and you can open up without even realizing how much you are revealing about yourself.

You may not be sure what you are even after, perhaps your online romantic liaisons are purely distraction or an aid to fantasy, but be cautious as you don't know what you are getting into. It may well be something special, however it could be very disappointed or ill advised.

Love and Marriage

Last month you needed to pay attention to communication and issues about respect. This month you have to address assumptions and narratives which have begun to develop in your relationship. What are the assumptions you make about each other, what have you grown to accept as unchangeable? It's time to challenge these assumptions and begin to talk about the things which have been brushed under the carpet. Mercury retrograde does complicate communication, however it also deepens it, and provides an opportunity to have more meaningful discussions about things which rarely come up, but which are always hanging like a cloud.

This is a chance to listen to things you don't want to hear and to talk about things that are uncomfortable and you may find it easier than you thought after the first nervous moments. You need to shatter your communication taboos and begin a whole new chapter in relating.

Sex

Fantasy is vital in sex this month, so going to the cinema or reading erotica together can stimulate intimate excitement. Good sex and the imagination are linked in June and so to be stimulated, you must be with someone who fires up your imagination in some way, either with seductive texting, storytelling or role play.

Dance can also bring about a magical atmosphere which improves sex. Another tip is sex which includes water i.e. in or at the sea, on a boat, in the shower etc.

Career

This is not the best month for a major new advertising campaign or promotions as they may either hit the wrong notes, or the timing may end up being bad. It can also be hard to quantify the results and the effectiveness of any pitch or slogan.

Be careful on your social media channels i.e. YouTube, twitter etc. that you observe copyright and do not misquote anyone. It's not so much about facts, it's about the context in which you present facts, and so be careful about the subtext of your comments and whether others could take them the wrong way.

It's a very good month for problem solving and detail work and you should not shy away from understanding the mechanism or the thinking behind any analysis. Now what I mean by that, is while it's easy to outsource a financial or marketing report, or get an employee to do some research for you, you should take nothing at face value, you need to interrogate the report or any data handed to you and make sure it makes sense and is relevant. This month you may need to check over the work of others or supervise your staff more scrupulously. At the end of the day, if something is important enough, do it yourself.

Key Dates

Venus goes direct on the 25th in Gemini and Mercury retrograde on the 18th in Cancer. The moon wanes from 5th the until the 21st making this a time of assessment, completion and planning, after the 21st is best for your new projects and for important business dates and launches. After the 21st is particularly good for property deals, home improvements and catering businesses. Research and writing reports is also favored. Be careful of borrowing money and running up debt. Not a good time to open a joint bank account or pool funds with business partners.

JULY 2020

Life

Mercury goes direct on the 12th of July and Venus is now direct in Gemini. This brings success with negotiations and communications. Long and short distance travel is now favored.

Education and training in the arts, especially fashion and design is a theme this month. Capricorn in architecture can also have success with new projects where you can demonstrate your flair. It's a time where you are able to express your creativity more freely.

Home initiatives like landscaping and redecorating or even building work can be exciting and welcome. Capricorn enjoy the feeling of demolishing the old and building something brand new from scratch. Often participating in the demolition itself can be therapeutic and you may enjoy tearing away old wallpaper or knocking down a wall to create a new interior.

There is a theme of purging in your life and whether you totally clear out your basement or restructure your business, you get emotional pleasure and release from doing this.

So pave the way for something new this month.

Money

Recent commitments need to be reviewed carefully, and plans for new business ventures and strategies need extra work.

You may not be quite as ready for a new level of financial responsibility than you thought, and so this is a good time to press pause and have a long hard think about what you may be taking on and if it really suits you.

A new job offer or promotion may not be a good fit and you could hold out just a tad longer to see if the offer either improves or a better one comes along. Don't take on a role with a large degree extra responsibility or longer hours unless it absolutely makes financial sense, or helps you up the ladder. Make sure you factor your personality into a job or money decisions, ask, "Is this me?"

Health

Good health in the next few weeks is knowing when enough is enough and when to get your mind off work and to allow your mind to wander to fantasy and lighter topics. Often we are so driven, we get guilty even to have thoughts unrelated to work – that is not good.

Capricorn are perhaps being too strict about diet and perhaps you need a few weeks off the routine, a chance to just forget about any self-imposed limitations or restrictions. Break some of your rule this month and it may feel good.

Romance

In romance, a sense of shared responsibility is vital, you won't be impressed with partners who cannot hold their side of the bargain. You are beginning to enter a critical phase in love, you are more observant and you tend to pick up on things that perhaps were invisible before and these may be bad habits, poor hygiene or quirky things about your partner which annoy you.

This month is a test of how you feel together day to day, and how you both react during arguments. It's a time where true colors are revealed and that's why it's a make or break month for new love, as you both end up being very honest, without even intending to, as all the emotions erupt, charm and diplomacy dissolve and your innate natures reveal themselves.

Love and Marriage

You can be defensive and touchy this month and you are more edgy emotionally. You may feel the need for a good argument to clear the air. Any recent tensions, or anything you have repressed lately will bubble up and demand expression.

It's a good time for total honesty and no beating about the bush.

It's a busy time on the home front and that can include renovations, bringing more work home, or having folks to stay and you and your partner need to be organized and pull together. Domestic life can descend into chaos and arguments can get out of control, the problem is that you and your partner are inclined to work against each other rather than to unite in a practical way to ensure the jobs at hand get done. Often there is excess emotion about matters which really require more pragmatism.

Sex

Developing camaraderie and the ability to laugh and also cry about your problems together is vital to the intimate side of your relationship – there must be a feeling of in it together and like you are both 50% stakeholders in the future of the family unit. If you feel your partner is either detached or not fully involved and committed, you will tend towards stormy relations and some dramatic outburst.

Career

This is a good period for improved morale and teamwork. If you are employed, you may experience better conditions and perks, or you may move to a more modern or well-equipped office. There is a feeling of enjoyment and satisfaction gained from work and new colleagues may add to the camaraderie or enjoyment of the job.

If you have changed job, you introduction to the new routines will go smoothly.

It's a great time to recruit and interview new staff, or arrange social events to improve staff bonding.

Relationships with your suppliers may be more contentious and you could have to introduce some strict new parameters or checks to ensure product quantity. You need to be wary of supplies trying to rip you off by reducing quality of product or service but increasing prices.

If you run a restaurant or guest house or have clients to your home, you may need to upgrade facilities in line with regulations or health and safety.

Key Dates

Mercury goes direct on the 12th of July. The moon wanes from the 5th to the 20th of July making this your knuckling down phase for implementing, understanding and planning. After the 20th is a good period for networking, conferences and introducing new technology. Social media campaigns are successful. Not a great month for new diets or exercise plans. New business ventures related to health or diet are not favored. Not a very successful time for work with children or animals. Not a good time for recruitment.

AUGUST 2020

Life

For the northern hemisphere, it's summer holidays and yet this is not necessarily a relaxing time for Capricorn who are highly energized and driven. This is a time not to kick back and be lazy, but to work hard on projects of personal importance. There is a great desire to seize control and to shape events and you have very strong ideas about things.

You may even be working to make a new start in life and you have to lay the foundations.

Even if you are on holiday you may favor an action holiday with sports, or outdoor activities which need stamina and fitness. You will probably spend part of you time off continuing home improvements, doing clear outs or even setting up a new business. It's a very impatient time when you just want to get on and see progress and the month is marked by urgency more than summer chillin'.

Money

A good month for problem solving, financial planning and correspondence relating to money. Your general desire for control comes to force financially as you cut losses and prune expenses. You have a great deal of mental clarity about what you really need and what you don't and that enables you to make ruthless choices.

In terms of money you manage for others, you may have to make judgement calls and show leadership as there may be many options, however you can rely on your innate abilities and talents to make the right choice.

In business, financial planning may occupy your mind and you are thinking ahead to the next few months and getting ready to make some quite big moves. It feels like it's coming together.

Health

While you thrive when you take on physical challenges, and while you also enjoy contact sports, you must be more cautious as injuries to bones and teeth are possible.

You have had quite a lot of sweet things lately, time to cut sugar and reduce carbs. This is an ideal month for protein rich foods and more vegetables.

Improve dental hygiene, brush and floss more often and get a check up to avert any dental issues.

Increase magnesium and calcium intake with vitamin D, and start reducing daily caffeine now if you are older and have any concerns about osteoporosis.

Romance

Love relationships and affection are very much a private matter. New romances may be kept secret or you may even play down your feelings in front of others. You are more protective of your private romantic life. You are unlikely to want to share details of your intimate life with friends or family.
A secret liaison can be quite a turn on right now.
Single Capricorn may quite enjoy the low level commitment of single life or in some cases you may welcome long distance or unconventional relationships that allow your freedom and which do not encroach on your private space.

Love and Marriage

You are very forceful and you want to take the lead in household decisions, you have a sense of purpose and a very strong idea about what is right, and so you are equipped and eager to make difficult decisions and to take the rap for them. It's a decisive time when you do what needs to be done despite any opposition.

Your partner is likely to be highly cooperative this month, he/she is easy going and helpful, however you in turn need to dial back the intensity and be a little more affectionate and also grateful as you often fail to show appreciation this month.

This is a good month for relationships to grow and improve in practical ways, however you may not always be able to relax enough to enjoy the fun and affectionate moments on offer. Try and switch off and find an oasis of calm for some tenderness with your partner.

Your partner tends to be the more wise and considered one, while you shoot from the hip this month, so let him/ her deal with other people for you.

Sex

I have spoken about control and you like to be in control this month, this can make you quite domineering and that may ruin the excellent potential for sex which exists this month. Find ways to relax and let go before you get into sex, it won't develop well if you are too wound up. Sex won't relax you, you have to relax first in order for it to go well for you both.

If your partner likes to be dominated sexually and he/she enjoys your aggressive side, great. However a more sensitive or gentle partner may find you a tad abrasive. You have high energy which is terrific for good sex, you just need to temper this with some affection and consideration and you are 'A' for away sexually.

Career

You have courage and focus and can push yourself to the limits. This month extra stamina and determination mean you can succeed at mental and physical tasks. You have endurance and you never say die, so you may claw victory from the jaws of defeat.

There are themes of destruction and renewal and you have the power to shape your life and bring about new opportunities, even if you feel as if you are in a desert of opportunity. There is always a solution to be found and you are able to dig deep.

You may enjoy taking on what seems impossible and this is a good month to fight for your rights or right a wrong. You feel guided by something powerful right now and that gives you added impetus.

This is a time to confront situations, face fears and set the record straight. You are purposeful and while it won't all go your way, you will risk arousing opposition as you are not for turning back.

Key Dates

The moon waxes from the 18th making this a green light period for new projects and business ventures unless they involve catering, hospitality or tourism. Not a good period for property deals or starting major changes to your home, rather finish what you have started.

SEPTEMBER 2020

Life

Mars goes retrograde on the 9th of September in Aries and this can put a damper on your plans, things slow down, but the message is to be more thoughtful and considered in your approach. Tearing things down may have felt like a release, but now you need to be totally sure that what you are building up is going to be a true reflection of what you need. This is a time to let the dust settle and take a moment of calm to reflect. It's a great time to utilize the imagination as a tool to envisage options, speed is not the be all and end all, nor is progress, what matters is getting your emotions, needs, priorities and aims aligned.

Nothing much can be achieved now unless your spiritual and ego wills are aligned, to make progress in this next phase of life, you need total honesty and the ability to understand your core needs and innate nature. Nothing you start now can succeed if the intentions conflict with who you are. It's not a period where you can conform to ideals or perspectives which are not your own. You need to be able to shut out the opinions of others and listen to your inner voice.

Money

This is a good time to talk to investors and make pitches for new investment.

Money spent this month should be on goals and projects already in progress rather than on anything new. Focus on your most important priorities and get those done first; chances are you will have ample time for checking out new opportunities and avenues for your business and also for hobbies outside of work.

If you are in business selling consumer goods, home decor or beauty products, you can be very successful; however, this month is great for all selling and promotion as your people skills and ability to make positive connections with others is favoured.

Health

Psychotherapy can be very effective right now and this is an opportune time to deal with anger issues. If you find that problems you had with your parents resurface with other authority figures, especially in relation to bullying, now is a good time to address that.

Acupuncture can be very helpful for relaxation and also addiction issues, but do get a recommendation from a friend or organization before you start treatment.

Romance

Love relationships which begin now are more intense and feelings run high; romance has a greater hold on you and it can tend to dominate your life and your thoughts, which can be quite distracting, but you are compelled to continue as a new lover holds a fascination for you. New love relationships have ups and downs from the starts and they tend to impact your life in strange ways. You may experience sudden jealousy and even possessiveness as this new relationship gets close quite quickly, and you may become quite irrational and easily threatened by potential problems which arise.

Love and Marriage

This is a good month for rational decisions and debate about money matters; it's an opportune time to work out finances and get your priorities straight for the next few months, unlike recent weeks, it's easier for you to work together.

Your relationships are more stable and steady this month and he sexual side is simulated, there is more opportunity to have sex as you feel relaxed and the pressure is off, allowing you to just enjoy the quiet moments and have a chance to develop into affection and intimacy.

You are more aware of factors which have shaped your relationship, and right now attitudes and ingrained behavior which tend to steer the relationship, and which often determines outcomes, is more obvious as it filters to the surface and is better understood by you. It is a time when suddenly things click in terms of your deeper understanding of your partner and this can help you to navigate the tense and awkward moments which arise more strategically and not so much in a knee jerk way.

Sex

Sex can go beyond the physical and can be an activity for creating greater awareness of each other and bringing you close again. Often tackling a sexual issue can be the way in which you address other issues like health and psychology, and so improving sex life can be the gateway to better health in general, as when you are honest about poor libido or low sexual vitality, and you look for solutions, those solutions have positive externalities.

Career

This is an excellent time for creative writing as Capricorn enjoy the solitude of writing as a pursuit and your imagination is very active. You may find writing fiction or writing on emotional and psychological issues interesting.

This is an excellent phase for research and investigation with respect to writing a report, essay or series of articles.

Your ability to negotiate, communicate and co-ordinate others is enhanced. This month is great for team leadership and organising group initiatives. September is ideal for those of you involved in careers where the ability to find solutions by balancing needs and extracting compromises is key.

Your ability to follow through can give you a very strong competitive advantage this month; you need to be decisive and keep the ball rolling on all your projects – this will keep you ahead of the competition. Try hard not to be distracted by issues that are not central to your work, try not to be drawn into office gossip and socialising at work as it can be counterproductive. Teamwork can hold you back and so work independently as much as possible, as others you are working with may be distracting.

Key Dates

The moon waxes from the 17th making this your fertile patch for new activities especially in connection the arts, music, design and alternative field.

OCTOBER 2020

Life

If you are in denial about your true feelings for situations or people, your subconscious can trigger events that can subversively challenge your conscious motives. Have you ever been really angry with someone but kept that anger in and pretended it was fine, then suddenly something unconnected happened, and that person exploded at you and the argument you tried to avoid happened anyway? Often our subconscious 'arranges' events that our conscious is trying to avoid – our subconscious is more in tune with what we really want and need while our conscious mind is often conditioned to act or behave in a certain way. Recognize your urges and react positively in addressing them rather than being complicit with fate in allowing others or events to precipitate what you shied away from.

Capricorn resolve and determination are high this month, and you have an excellent sixth sense about what is needed or how to manage people in each and every situation. You are highly attuned to current events and trends and are the first to get news through on the grapevine, meaning that you can be one step ahead of the pack. Your intuition and logical powers are at their peak, and you can act more decisively than usual; you are capable of making some extremely tough decisions, and even though you may sometimes choose to do things the hard way, you will get the best results. You have guts, fire and determination, and you won't wimp out on anything – you are there to win.

Money
This is a month of increasing financial security and financial progress. It is a good time to start a new investment plan or open a savings account. Time spent planning your money and thinking about pensions and cost-effective borrowing is time wisely spent.
You may be trying to arrange finance for big purchase, i.e. house or car or putting in offers – this is a good time to judge the market and get a really good deal without compromising on quality.

This month is excellent for negotiating in money matters and driving a hard bargain. There is much information to take on right now whether you are investing, learning, buying something complex, etc. and at times you may feel mentally overloaded, but you are able to cope as long as you tackle things systematically, not with a blitz approach.

Health

Good health is about understanding key issues better. Do your own research and get advice from a variety of sources. Health is not 2+ 2= 4, it's often way more complicated, nuanced and highly individual, and so only you can know your own body completely, thus the more you learn about your treatments and share your personal information with your doctor, the better results you can get from the medical professionals.

Always try to find information on how certain pharmaceutical drugs interact with alternative medicine with alcohol or with over the counter drugs, as often they work against each other. Remember to avoid grapefruit juice when on medication, especially for the heart.

Romance

People will find it easy to relate to and open up to you this month; you are very receptive to emotions and eager to be helpful. Your intelligence and ability to make good conversation will open doors to new love – you may find that you click with someone with similar artistic interests. Love tends towards an intellectual side – you are unlikely to be attracted to someone who does not stretch you mentally or does not share your interests. Opposites attract is not the key for love in October – new romantic partners must be on the same page as you when it comes to interests, mentality and intelligence. If lovers just want a passing fling, that will not be for you.

Love and Marriage
In love, your ability to be strong, resolute and loyal is very important right now – you will have to be the rock, and to a degree you will have to keep a lid on your own emotions and be tough to provide direction in the relationship and support for your partner.
Values are very important to you right now, and you will be firm on setting an example to your children via the way you and your partner communicate, resolve issues and react to problems.
You will want to show your children the virtues of being generous and giving, especially to those beyond your social circle.

Sex

Sex is about luxury and comfort, so it's a time for caviar and champagne, or whatever you enjoy most. Sex has to be indulgent or you won't get turned on, so make it a treat and spoil or treat yourselves in order to get in the mood.

Career

The pace of this month is very fast, and it can be very good for travelling in connection with conventions, sales or promotional activities. Travel, especially national travel is a feature of your life and can bring you success and enjoyment.

October is favorable for all study, learning and any mental activity involving numbers. If you run a business, then this month is perfect for honing business skills, and that could mean learning more about accounting, management techniques or investment options, to enhance your understanding and the way you do business. You should not look for quick fixes regarding ideas that are very simple and offer amazing results; this month is more about a serious and determined effort to understand your job, your business or your industry better, and thus to have a more thorough approach to what you do.

Key Dates

The moon waxes from the 17th making this your fertile patch for new activities especially in connection with charities and humanitarian work. Political activism is favored.
Theatre events, festivals and music events are favored. A good time for businesses involving the care industry.

NOVEMBER 2020

Life

Mercury goes direct on the 3rd and Mars on the 13th. This means that you are coasting down the road again and can put your foot on the accelerator with a feeling of the wind on your hair.

You are able to plan and you will be quite excited about the options open to you, you are eager to embrace technology and get on board with new innovative methods if working or in terms of hobbies.

Fulfilling your dreams right now is linked to embracing change and not sticking to traditional methods. You should strive to be highly individualistic and to achieve things that mark you out as unique - you must carve your own path rather than just follow others and this means being daring and adopting practices that are 'out there'.

This is a very powerful time mentally for Capricorn, you can literally think yourself into or out of problems. You mind is both incisive and highly observant, and you have an ability to project your thoughts out into the world so that they can manifest. The problem however, is that you are likely to be suspicions and you can almost bring out the devious side of others if you chose to focus on it. If you believe someone is out to get you, you will almost engineer a situation where that is confirmed to you. However, if you can focus on positive thoughts and believe that others are going to help you, then they will end up proving to you that they are of assistance. Once you have the thought in your head, you have the outcome and so make sure it is a positive and healthy thought.

Money

Money making linked to your true calling or long held ambitions is favored. If you work as a shop manager, but write in your spare time and dream of getting a publishing deal this is the time to get serious as this is a month where such dreams can become reality if you are audacious and back yourself and go after them. It is not only about writing, that is just an example, anything which inspires you at a deep level and makes you feel happy and alive is more likely to be successful in monetary terms and in terms of winning recognition.

Health

Capricorn should work on improving flexibility: dynamic stretching i.e. lunges, squats, push ups and jumping jacks can do more for you than long hold stretches especially in terms of warming up. Hill walking, going up and down stairs and some energetic gardening where you dig and shovel are also great forms of exercise that are cheap and accessible but which improve flexibility and fitness at most ages.

Massage can be very helpful in breaking up knots in muscles which impair movement

Romance

Capricorn are focused on inner growth and also on greater self-awareness. If you are in a new relationship, any lack of depth or phoniness in your partner will become glaring and something that will call the relationship into question. Capricorn have an eye on the future and that is why you need to be able to see yourself with the person you are with now, in the future, or why would you bother carrying on putting time into this relationship.

Love and Marriage
This month can be rather like a karmic boomerang, where seeds that may have been sown in the past, in terms of sacrifices made, greater understanding sought, improving communication or a good deed done, now start to germinate into tangible positives for your relationship.

You are highly observant this month and will pay attention to everything which can bring out that suspicious side of you and you may end up giving your partner the 9th degree over something quite innocent. Reading between the lines can cause more trouble and stress than it is worth and so sit back and relax, sometimes there is nothing there to be interpreted, life can be what is seems, it does not have to be one giant murder mystery.

Sex
Sexual interactions step up a notch and Capricorn are more ardent and active in the bedroom. You can be a little impatient, you tend to want what you want when you want it and you are not all that compromising.

Sex is all about boosting the ego of your partner; you may have to do some subtle coaxing, but you need to bring them out of their shell and uncover that sexual beast within them.

Career

You may work more with younger people and they may be key to your success. You may need to consult more with the under 25s to develop products or strategy for your business. In terms of employment, you may be moved to a position where you must understand the trends, needs and preferences of the youth for marketing or targeting purposed. It may be that you have to adjust a website or your PR to address green issues, or any other political issue that is close to the heart of the younger generation. There is an element of virtue signaling this month, which is a necessary evil depending on how you feel about woke issues. Whether you are 'woke' or not, you need to know what woke is and how to accommodate progressive attitudes in your work.

You will need to have an increased presence on social media and it's not enough to be doing what everyone else is doing and so you may need to be more controversial.

Your ability to blend in and adapt to new situations, making emotional connections with new people fast, is an asset in business and you can expand your networks quickly.

Key Dates

Mercury goes direct on the 3rd and Mars on the 13th. The moon waxes from the 15th meaning that you are all ready, get set go and can proceed at pace with end of year activities. An excellent period for new starts, image changes and cosmetic and dental work. New romance, childbirth and teaching children is favored. Ventures connected to games, entrainment and sports are favored. A good period for interviews and job applications. New starts and also competitive activities are favored.

DECEMBER 2020

Life

This is a wonderful month for those who have been feeling hemmed in or constrained, to finally bloom and take center stage. You are most successful this month when you have used 2020 to crystallize your goals and chose those which most align to your inner calling.

You can forge new alliances or make new friends this month who are similar to you in terms of where you are in terms of personal evolution and they quickly become allies.

This month is an excellent time for taking your creative projects off the drawing board and into the limelight.

December is ideal for playing around with ideas in your head and just seeing where they take you – imagination can be used to increase your optimism by envisioning positive outcomes. Time to break any unlucky streak by focusing on what you did right rather than wrong and building on that.

Money

Your plans are possibly greater than your budget and yet you are determined to find ways to creatively make money go further so that you can invest more in exciting plans or in special events to spoil yourself.

Savvy and business minded, this can be a strong period for gathering new money-making ideas and setting clear goals with a thorough game plan.

This month, money can be made by teaching. You do not have to be a teacher as such, you may have a specialist interest or skill, which would enable you to coach children or young people part-time. You may have done ballet or played piano to a high level, now may be the time to pass on those skills to others and make some cash.

Health

Your health gets a boost and you have added energy to achieve the extra work you have right now. You should however take on extra nutrition, so make sure you eat more bananas, avocados, sweet potato and pumpkin.

Don't get roped into anything you do not feel up for – if you have a bad feeling about something then listen to that instinct and do not be cajoled into anything by friends who could have very different needs and desires to you.

Romance

While you are happy go lucky and easy going in love, you are also a little lazy about making definite arrangements or going out, and so a great period for chilling with some prosecco or a hot chocolate in the garden or by the fire and enjoying the December heat or cold depending on where you are. Extreme weather tends to excite you romantically and so experiencing the great outdoors where you are more exposed to weather can make you feel sexy and romantic.
Capricorn are in a very romantic mood in December and you are inspired by the higher, more spiritual aspects of love i.e. the willingness to sacrifice, seeing the person for what they are spiritually rather than materially, love despite the odds, love in the face of opposition. In many ways love is more exciting for Capricorn when there is opposition or a sense that you are saving someone, or being saved. Sometimes your attitudes to love are not very practical, in fact you are not motivated by logic and reason when you meet new people, you are motivated by feeling and raw emotion. You will also tend to be highly idealistic in love and have unusual romances which begin in extraordinary ways.

Love and Marriage

More freedom is what you need in your established unions: that freedom can be physical (i.e. spending more time on your hobbies) or mental (being more vocal about your opinions and sexual needs). You will crave spontaneity and so your partner needs to surprise you and go with the flow. You will demand changes to relationships to improve understanding and also inject more novelty and excitement. Relationships where Capricorn are involved with someone very stubborn and set in their ways will suffer.

Sex

While you felt rather emotional the past few months and expressed that sexually and in terms of arguments and domination, this month you are far more balanced and even tempered in your love life. This is a good month for working on strengthening the sexual relationship – good communication is needed, working on problems and addressing the key concerns you both have is vital.

This is a very good time for new same-sex relationships, partly because same-sex relationships are often transformative and part of a significant life theme about identity and Capricorn are more in tune with core identity this month.

Career

You may get the chance to travel to a far flung place for a temporary work placement or you may travel to do charity or humanitarian work. Travel in relation to charity work may involve travel to particularly desperate places where poverty is an issue, but not to areas which are war torn.

Long haul travel is highly likely for work purposes or to research a new place to move to in the New Year.

You are eager to learn and discover things for yourself; standard answers will not have relevance for you and may feel wrong – there is a strong need to get closer to certain problems or issues to experience them for real and draw your own conclusions.

Positive changes in your life start with developing new long rage goals; goals that inspire you and make you want to get out of bed and make the best of whatever situation you find yourself in. The Jupiter Saturn conjunction on the eclipse is a highly fortuitous sign for Capricorn and heralds a year in 2021 of prosperity and fulfilment as well as success, so certainly a time to be optimistic and to think big.

Key Dates

The moon waxes from the 14th to the 29th making this a proactive, prosperous and lucky phase where you have excellent results in terms of getting recognition, support and encouragement. You are lucky with anything last minute. Discipline and systematic work pays off. Investment in emerging industries and science is favored. Philosophical activities, charity work and social work is favored. Long distance travel by sea is lucky, as are attending retreats and spas. Friends can be made out of enemies. Helping the under-privileged is successful.

THANK YOU SO MUCH FOR PURCHASING THIS BOOK – HAVE A WONDERFUL 2020 AND 2021.